Poetry & Wisdom

Dwayne Wong (Omowale)

ISBN: 1477616225
ISBN-13: 978-1477616222

DEDICATION

To Dwayne, Marcia, Danielle, and Dominic.

CONTENTS

Acknowledgments

ACKNOWLEDGMENTS

Special thanks to Tracy Cherubin for the cover art

REVOLUTION

Wake up

It's time

We have been asleep

For far too long

Slavery

Colonialism

Oppression

Starvation

It is time for revolution

It is time for liberation

We cannot afford to remain silent

To remain complacent

So many problems in the world

So stand up and fight

Come together now

And let us unite

I say we need a revolution

I say we need some change

Men, women, and children

Have suffered too long

And the pressure on our backs

It is much too strong

So come

Let us build a revolution

Let us unite

Let us change our situation

And end this plight

We need revolution

So let the revolution come

DEEP RHYMES

My rhymes are heavy and deep

How heavy and deep

I dropped my rhyme book once

And it shattered the concrete

DAY MASH UP

It's morning

Dropped my cup

Coffee spill

Day mash up

RODNEY

Banned him from Jamaica
Killed him in Guyana
But you can't stop the people
As we march to our liberation

SLAVE FETE

Boi if yuh see dance
If yuh see prance
All a dem jus' fete an' ting
An' nah care wha de nex' day a bring

Nah worry wid toil an' whip
Nah worry 'bout none slave ship
Dem jus' dance an' smile
Dem jus' wan' fuh be wil'

If yuh see slave fete
Me neva see ting so yet

Translation:

You should have seen the dancing
And the prancing
All of the slaves partied
And did not care about the next day

They did not worry about toil or the whip
They did not worry about any slave ships
They just danced and smiled
They just wanted to act wild

You should have seen the slave party
I have never seen anything like it

MARCUS GARVEY

Where did you go
Mighty Marcus
Where's your dreams
Where's your hopes

We watched in admiration
When you were in your prime
We cheered and joined up
For the Black Star Line

You gave us hope
You gave us pride
We flaunted our African identity
And never tried to hide

Well, where did you go
Marcus
Marcus Garvey
You made us stand tall
With pride on our face
We listened eagerly
When you said
"Up You Mighty Race"

We looked to Africa
We looked for a Black king
Because your words told us
That we were something

From Jamaica to Africa
You made the Negro world rise
How we loved it
Rastas said you prophesized

Well, where are you Marcus?
You said you went home
Home to make Africa free
So that all of Africa may know
The Honorable Marcus Garvey

BLACK STAR

Look east
Where we shall rise
Stand upright
And focus your eyes

Gaze upon the Black Star
The star of our liberation
That star that will uplift
The entire African nation

UBUNTU

I am

Because we are

And if you fall

We all fall

AFRICA SHALL RISE

I woke up
One morning
And I saw
Great kings

I met Mansa Musa
As we traded in gold
The march of the Zulus
I did behold

I witnessed queens
Nzinga ruling with ease
Heading her army
To fight the Portuguese

I saw a proud people
Much to my surprise
And on that day I knew
Africa shall rise

THE WISE MAN AND THE FOOL

The wise man studies
So that he may speak
The fool speaks
On that which he has never studied

HARDSHIPS

I asked Harriet Tubman
How she got free
Hardship and struggle
Is what she told me

Went to Mandela
And I heard his tale
He spent much time
Locked up in jail

Toussaint L'Ouverture
Suffered much strife
And Louis Delgrès
Gave up his life

Thomas Sankara was grim
As he said his piece
How he had to suffer
To make oppression cease

Malcolm X was in jail
And made me understand
Before he was educated
He was a conman

Cuffy took blows
To escape the plantation
Hardships I knew
Was his situation

Paul Bogle was silent
But I knew the truth
Struggle was the plan
That he had to execute

I heard tales of hardships

So believe me
I do not expect
Anything to come easy

DEM A VEX

Dem a vex
Dem a mad
Dem bruk up fence
An' mash up yard

Dem vex with poverty
Dem vex with starvation
Dem done with misery
Dem done with sufferation

Translation:

They are vex
They are mad
They destroyed a fence
And destroyed a yard

They are vex with poverty
They are vex with starvation
They are done with misery
They are done with suffering

IDENTITY THEFT

Lost my name
And my language too

I've forgotten who I was
Where I was
What I did

I look to history
But I'm not there

I look to the media
But it's nothing good
Nothing flattering
Nothing noteworthy

They say I'm a savage
Dwelling in jungles
Devouring human flesh

Scientists
Doctors
Thinkers
Scholars

Those are things
Not reserved for me
Those are things
Observed in European history

This is not amnesia
That much I know

No, this is theft
I've been robbed

JUMBIE MAN

Was a col' col' night
An' it was jus' me alone
Sittin' 'pon me chair
Writin' inna me home

Suddenly me hear a growl
Nex' me hear a crash
Me get up quick
An' if yuh see dash

Me ran fuh de door
An' guess wha me a see
Me jump up real fas'
An' try fuh escape quickly

Stanin' nex' to me window
With claws 'pon he han'
Was one shadowy figure
Dat dem a call de jumbie man

Translation:

It was a very cold night
And I was alone
Sitting in my chair
Writing in my home

Suddenly I heard a growl
And then I heard a crash
I got up quick
You should have seen me dash

I ran for the door
And guess what I saw
I jumped up very fast
And tried to escape quickly

Standing next to my window
With claws on his hand
Was a shadowy figure
That people call the jumbie man

THESE HANDS

By these skillful hands
Pyramids rose
In Egypt and Nubia

These brilliant hands
Built Timbuktu
And built Songhai

These weary hands
Picked cotton and cut sugar cane
For the Americans, Dutch, British
French and Portuguese

These strong hands
Fought for liberation

These powerful hands
Are the reason we survive

GREED

You can consume
But never consume enough

You can buy
But never buy enough

You can own
But never own enough

You can accumulate
But never accumulate enough

You can have enough
But never have enough

THE TRAPPINGS OF FAME

Imagine it
Having fame
Everywhere you go
People know your name

Everywhere you turn
People want to be your friend
To have so much fame
And never be lonely again

Yet despite the fame
Can you really be you
Do people love your fame
Or do people really love you

I WAS A KING

I was a king

The ruler of my land

Now I am a slave

My original language I don't understand

I was a free man

In charge of my life

Now I am a slave

Living in strife

But I remember

I remember who I am

I remember I was a king

Before I left my land

WORDS

Words have power
Power to kill
And power to heal
Power to destroy
And the power of appeal

Words can be sharp
As sharp as a knife
And words can be cheerful
And give meaning to life

Words have power
Not to be taken lightly
So when you pick your words
Choose them wisely

DEATH OF A FEDERATION

They say they want to federate
But then they disagree
And the whole federation
Just began to disintegrate

Same slave ship
But different island
So why we cannot federate
Is a thing I cannot understand

CORRUPTION

Dem mek promises
When election year come
But is dem get de riches
An' de people does get none

Yuh swear 'pon Bible
Is you wey tek oath
Yuh promise honesty
But lie fuh de vote

Corrupt politician
Is time yuh understan'
Yuh corruption an' lies
Is killin' de common man

Translation:

They make promises
When election year comes
But they get the riches
And the people get none

You swear on the Bible
Is you that takes the oath
You promise honesty
But lie for the vote

Corrupt politician
It is time you understand
Your corruption and lies
Are killing the common man

UNITY AFRICAN

One ship to America
One ship to Jamaica
One ship to Haiti
One ship to Trinidad

One ship to Guyana
One ship to Brazil
One ship to Barbados
One ship to Grenada

One ship to St. Vincent
One ship to Cuba
One ship to Antigua
One ship to St. Croix

We are the Diaspora
Spread throughout the land
Now it is time for unity
For every African

MASSA DAY DONE

After centuries of oppression
The era has begun
The people will be free
And massa day done

THE RACE

Waiting, calmly in the blocks

There is peace, silence, and serenity

The sprinter lowers his head

And closes his eyes

Envisioning his task

Four years of practice

Comes down to this single moment

Then the gun goes off

Without thinking he reacts

There is an explosion out of the blocks

A violent yet calm explosion

The sprinter stays focused

As he speeds to the finish line

Paying no attention to his left nor his right

He runs the race he practiced

The race he has dreamed up

Seconds later he crosses the line

And reaches the glory of gold

FUZZY WUZZY

The British came
To conquer your land
But they did not know
The fighting spirit of the African

They called you Fuzzy Wuzzy
But you were so bold to dare
To confront the British Empire
And to break their infantry square

DRUGS AND ADDICTION

I control you
Have you seen yourself lately?
Your life is falling apart
But you cannot escape me

Because of me
You lost your family

I stole your wealth
Because you need me
I robbed your health
But you cannot see it plainly

WHAT IS FREEDOM

What is freedom?
It is a thing dreamt of by slaves
And taken for granted by the free

The Founding Fathers wanted freedom
And they spoke of liberty
But history books will tell you
They held Africans in slavery

The American Revolution was fought
For liberty
But only for people
Of a specific ancestry

America was born
But women could not vote

The revolution was for freedom
Or so we are told
But what of the Native Americans
Whose lands the Founding Fathers stole?

And voting was restricted
To wealthy white men alone
One could not vote
If land they did not own

If the Revolution won freedom
Why did Martin Luther King march?
What were the Panthers fighting for
If the Revolution made us free

So when they speak of freedom
I question their concept of liberty
The Revolution was freedom for some
For others it was slavery

UNCLE TOM

Your people are bawling
Mr. Tom
Yet you fight for people
Who do not respect you

You sit by and watch
As your people suffer
And all you want is to enrich yourself

Your community suffers
Your people are in pain
Mr. Tom are you not vex?
Are you not enraged?

Did you forget the ships
The whips
And the plantations
Did you forget
The destruction of African nations

Mr. Tom
Stand up
Fight
Do something courageous
For once in your life

WHEN I WAS A SAVAGE

When I was a savage
I was free
But some Christians came
To civilize me

When I was a savage
I was free
Now I'm civilized
And trapped in slavery

A NORMAL DAY

I wake up slow
And peep from my window
To see the city below

I see a homeless man
With a tan
Whisky bottle in hand
He could barely stand

Next, I look to Gar
The owner of a local bar
He sits in his car
Smoking a cigar
With the door ajar

Next I see a bloody pipe
And a busted street light
From the vicious fight
Last night

Just another normal day
In the city I call home

GUN MAN

Gun man
Me beg yuh
Fuh give up yuh crime
Continue 'pon yuh pat'
An' yuh go dead in no time

Put down yuh gun
An' jus' a pick up a pen
Instead a figtin' battle
Jus' a write out problem

Translation:

Gun man
I beg you
To give up your crime
Continue on your path
And you will be dead in no time

Put down your gun
And just pick up a pen
Instead of fighting battles
Just write out your problems

FREE AT LAST, BUT NOT QUITE YET

I beat Napoleon in Haiti
And made the British respect me in Jamaica
I fought for Palmares in Brazil
I fought with Buddhoe
And ran away with Harriet Tubman
They hanged me with Sam Sharpe
And burned me with Makandal

They gave me the Emancipation Proclamation
And I cried free at last
Yet achieving freedom
Remains a daunting task

DR. KING

Dr. King wanted peace

So they killed him with violence

SMILE

I smile
When things go well
But it is rather hard to smile
When things go to hell

MY POEMS

My poems will open your eyes
You will read their words
And it will make you wise

I speak of the struggle
Of a people's history
The quest of a people
To escape misery

My poems contain knowledge
Like the library of Alexandria
Or the books of Timbuktu

My poems are like weapons
For the oppressed
And hope for the hopeless
And those born with less

I VEX

I write this
To make you know
How it is
People does vex me so

I tell no lie
This is no false pretense
But I vex with people
And their nonsense

APARTHEID

You came to my land
I made you a guest
You stole my land
And left me powerless

I fought with the Xhosa
And the Zulu
But in the end was conquered
And my governments you overthrew

You jailed Nelson Mandela
And Robert Sobukwe as well
Murdered Steve Biko
And by an assassin Chris Hani fell

Give back my land
And let my people be free
I will crush apartheid
Before that system crushes me

DEPRESSED ME

I caught myself
Watching myself
Watching me
And did not know
Who it was that I did see

Who is this mysterious
Miserable
Depressed person watching me

When I smile
My reflection smiles as well
But with a weak grin
I want to make a real smile
But the smile in the mirror
Is not so genuine

Who is this person
Watching me
And when I feel happiness
The mirror reflects my misery

BRIBE

The politician swore in
And promised to govern honestly
But his opinion changed
When he saw the money

JUSTICE

How can justice
Be preserved
When justice is
Selectively reserved

IDI AMIN

A dictator
Oppressing a land
A people fallen victim
To a mad man

Coming to power
In a foreign supported coup
A man who wrecked his own nation
By the time he was through

He called himself a conqueror
A conqueror of the British Empire
But he was a farce
It was against Tanzania;
other Africans
That he sent his soldiers to march

BLUES

I sing blues
Because I have felt the strain
I am an African
So I sing the blues
Because I have faced pain
I sing the blues
Because I have stood in the rain
I sing blues
Because it keeps me sane

LIARS IN OFFICE

It is tradition
Presidents swear an oath
The office of Honest Abe
And Washington
Who never told a lie
Yet this is also an office
Which liars occupy

Richard Nixon
A criminal liar
Do you remember his fate
How he was quick to resign
Right after Watergate

One Bush said no new taxes
But this was untrue
His son, another Bush
Spoke of weapons of mass destruction
But when he invaded Iraq
The facts came out
And he took his claim back

Ronald Regan
For hostages
He traded weapons with Iran
But claimed he did not
And like Nixon
Reagan had a similar fate
But rather than water
His was a debategate

Then there is Bill
Who lied plainly
When he said he had no relations
With Miss Lewinski

RISE QUEEN

Rise up my queen
And take your place
As a woman of dignity
And much grace

FLOWING DOWN THE NILE

Flowing down the Nile
Where Kemet once stood
Where Africans ruled in glory
As they rightfully should

LEAVE HER ALONE

If she means you no well
Do not fall for her deceit
Understand her intentions
Before you bow at her feet

SELF-HATE

They give you an image
An image that is not you
And you have to fit that image
If it is the last thing you do

Spending so much money
But you still cannot hide
No amount of material success
Alters the hatred inside

COME TO THE GHETTO

Come to the ghetto
To see horrors and pain
Come to the ghetto
And you will never wish to come back again

WHEN I FOUND MY ROOTS

I remember when
I found my roots

I found myself
I found my pride
I came away
With a new confidence inside

I grew up
Knowing little of the Caribbean
And much less of Africa

I knew Africans were cannibals
And uncivilized
But the greatness of my ancestors
Was a thing I did not realize

DEAR LEADER

Dear leader,
This is a message
From the common man
We are tired of taxes
And strain
I hope you understand

POVERTY AND WEALTH

The rich are on top
Living so well
The poor are in the gutter
Living in hell

The rich are living large
Drinking champagne
The poor are living low
And feeling the strain

GRANDMOTHER'S STRUGGLES

When days are rough
And I am feeling blue
I always remember
What my grandmother went through

Being taken from Africa
Her native land
And being molested
By some strange man

How she fought
And resisted everyday
How much she sacrificed
So that I can prosper today

CRIMINAL

Who is the true criminal?
The one who commits the crime
Or the one that creates the conditions
That reduces one to crime

TAKE ME BACK HOME AGAIN

I can wander
And travel so many lands
But I want to go back home
Once again

TUPAC

Remember Tupac Amaru
The ruler of the Inca state
Before the Spanish came
And executed him swiftly

Remember Tupac Amaru II
A man who fought for his land
And along with his wife
Paid the ultimate price

I MUST WRITE

When I see my people's plight
You know I must write

I must write on poverty
And oppression

I must write on suffering
And starvation

When I see my people's plight
You know I must write

DIS MAN

If yuh see dis man
Wid one Bible inna he 'and
He a preach de word
An' a call fuh de Lawd
But me know de fact
Dis man is one fraud

HONESTY

They say honesty will set you free
But when I was honest
They came
And crucified me

When will we realize
This society
Is addicted to lies

EVERYTHING WAS BACKWARDS

Understand please, morning one up woke I
Lie no is this and
Backwards was everything
Sing grass the heard I
Fly to began grass the and
Dirt the from grew birds the as

Backwards was everything
Lie no is this
Teeth my rubbed I
Eye my brushed I and

Breakfast my drank I
Juice my ate and
Socks my tied I
Loose laces the left and

Work to went I
Boss the was I where
Way the on
Horse a milking farmer a saw I

Confused was I
Lie no is this
Backwards was everything
Why know not did I and

SAVE YOUR LOVE

This woman came up to me
And promised me her love
But in return she wanted my wealth
So I told her
Save your love

THE STORY OF MY WASHINGTON

I do not disagree
That there was a Washington
Who was a great freedom fighter
But I am not speaking of George

The Washington of which I speak
His name was Madison Washington
He fought and he prevailed
So I am here to tell his tale

The year was 1841
The ship was called the *Creole*
Packed with more than 100 slaves
Washington and the others rebelled

They captured the ship
And sailed to Nassau
Where the Black Man was free
And thus this Washington
Won his liberty

THE SOUND OF THE CONGO

Listen close
And you will hear
The sound of the Congo
That I hold so dear

In my rhythms
In my speech
The sound of the Congo
Is a thing I can't teach

KKK

Killing Africans
Keeping us down
Kicking us around

FREE PRESIDENT

I won't celebrate a first Black President
Or even a Prime Minister
I've had Nkrumah, Obama, and Williams
Burnham as well

Now I want the Black President
That is right for me
The one who will
Finally set me free

WHO CREATED BLACK POWER

Who created Black Power
And why?
Let's look at the facts

Don't look at Malcolm X
Or Stokely Carmichael
Don't look to the Black Panthers
Or Huey Newton

Slavery
Racism
Colonialism
Apartheid
They created Black Power

I RECALL 9/11

I recall that day
When they attacked
Towers fell
People died

We went to war
But what lessons did we learn
In the quest for peace

IF BABYLON SHOULD FALL

If Babylon should fall
The people would dance
And rejoice

They would yell out
Our captivity is over
We are now free

Be gone Babylon
Fall and be gone
So we can be free

FREE THE MIND

Free the mind
And the rest
Shall be free

Strengthen the mind
And the rest
Shall be strengthened

Educate the mind
And the rest
Shall be educated

MAKING OF CRIMINALS

When you give children poor models
Or when you give them poor schools
You give them poor education
And make them into poor fools

You promote violence
You promote greed and material wealth
You promote drugs and drinking
And celebrate poor health

The family unit crumbles
And the job market as well
You put them in a situation
Where it is death or a prison cell

Situations like this
Criminals do make
When their options are limited
And their lives are at stake

A DREAM

It came to me
In a dream one day
So I picked up a pen
And I began to write
Of what my dream
Told me that night

EVERY BROTHER IS NOT A BROTHER

When I look at the situation
The truth I'm forced to see
Every brother is not a brother
And that is the reality

HITLER MARCHED

Hitler marched
And waged war
A lunatic
With a task
Killing Jews
Plunging Europe
Into war
Into confusion
And destruction

Hitler marched
And Europe
And the world
Was never the same
Keep a close watch
Because one day
Hitler may
March again

NO NIGGAS

There are no niggas
Not really
No
But there are Africans
This much I know

I'S DE POLICE

Yuh seh yuh nah know me
Well now yuh go see
I's de police
An' me go bring brutality

Armed with me gun
An' baton in han'
Me go gie yuh licks
Till yuh cyan stan'

You seh I's a brute
But I does serve you
An' if yuh question me
Yuh go get licks too

Translation:

You say you don't know me
Well now you will see
I am the police
And I will bring brutality

Armed with my gun
And baton in hand
I will give you licks (blows)
Until you can't stand

You say I am a brute
But I serve you
And if you question me
You will get licks too

JOHN HENRY REVISITED

You know the classic tale
John Henry
The steel driving man
He beat a steam powered hammer
And died after he won
But I say
He should have taken his hammer
And beaten his way to freedom

VOODOO POEMS

My poetry is like voodoo
Or so I am told
Because when people read my verses
They are under my control

JUMBIE POET

They say
I must be a jumbie
Because I am so mystical
With my poetry

I must be a jumbie
Because I write so well
So they came with some handcuffs
And locked me in a jumbie cell

THE MASK

If you wear a mask
Be cautious
Because no one ever knows
When the day will come
When the mask falls
And their face is exposed

BLACK WOMAN

It has always been me and you
Black woman
I could never forsake you
For you sustained me through the years
So I must apologize
When I make you shed tears

ONCE UPON A TIME

Story books begin a fictional story with "once upon a time"

Politicians begin a fictional story with "if elected"

THE MINISTER

They say the minister
Was brought to court
On corruption charges

But the case was settled
The minister made it clear
He's got connections
And knows people
So he has no fear

TUBMAN

I wish I could follow her
To freedom
But alas
I am still a slave
And Ms. Tubman
Is so courageous
And so brave

JEWEL

The most expensive jewel

That I own

Is not on my neck

Or my wrists

It is my mind

ME VS. ME

I know you may think me strange
But my head is well
So listen closely
To the story I must tell
I want to make this clear
And I hope you see
I have a rival
And the rival's me

Every day I wake up early
And get ready for my job
But myself is a lazy slob
Listen close
And you will know my hate
Every day I wake up early
And myself makes me late

Then the other night
The thing that started the fight
I went out gambling
I lost some money
But had mostly success
But myself gambled some more
And lost all the rest

So I am telling you
And I know I am right
I will encounter myself
In one final fight
It's either him
Or it's me
But we cannot exist together
As one peacefully

PRIDE

Have some pride
Mr. African
And drop that skin bleaching cream
Out of your hand

NEW REALM

Some creatures
Took me away last night
To a new realm
That I had never seen
Except in my sleep
Whenever I dream

I saw children happy
And the people were so polite
I paid close attention
And saw not a single fight

There was a certain peace
And no one was poor
It was a strange world
I have only dreamt of before

Sadly, I left the next week
But I still think of that realm
And see it every night
In my sleep

HAMPTON

One night you were sleeping
Safe in your bed
But your enemies were cowards
And shot you in the head

DEFEAT

The bitter
Taste
Of defeat
Will bring
Anyone down
To their feet

But there is
A lesson
In all things
And strength
Is an experience
That defeat brings

MOYIBI

Moyibi
Is what I would call you
Because you stole my heart

MOSES

Moses return
Your people are
Captive once more
Under Egypt's grip
We cannot stand
Under so much oppression

MY DOMAIN

Welcome to my domain
Where I rule as king
This pen is my weapon
Like a sword to wield
And the page is the battlefield
Where I command words
Towards battle
And the reader is conquered

TELL ME LIES

Tell me lies
To spare my heart
Or be brutally honest
And tear me apart

PEOPLE ARE CRAZY

People are crazy
I don't understand
A man so poor
And having to beg
But he gets a paycheck
And wastes that money on irrelevant things
Such as new gadgets and gold rings

And a rich man would have plenty
But he cannot have enough
He's got a mansion
With 50 rooms
And he still wants more stuff

FOOLISH MAN

This is the story of a foolish man
Who has plenty women
All over town
East and West
North and South
Plenty women
All about

Not very selective with his women
And often carless
Little did he know
His last woman was the La Diablesse

He met her in the night
And was enchanted by her smile
He began to think of nothing but bliss
Yet another woman to add to his list

But his sexual conquest
Was spoiled when he realized
That night it was to see
The fear in his eyes

The woman pulled up her dress
To reveal her cow foot
The man shrieked in fear
For he knew
The La Diablesse
Would kill him too

This is a warning
To all foolish men
When you pick your women
Be very wise
Or it could be you too
That the La Diablesse fries

DUTCH MAN'S REVENGE

There is a legend
In Guyana
So please listen close
To the story of a vengeful
Dutch man's ghost

The Dutch man was a planter
Who owned many slaves
But was killed in the uprising
In the Cuffy days

But he wanders around
His spirit escaped hell
And he torments the people
For this is what he does well

THE MOON GAZER

It was a dark night
And the moon was full
They ran in terror and in fear
For they all knew
That the Moon Gazer was near

SLAVE UPRISING

I ran to the master
To let him know
The slaves are uprising
And seeking revenge

They burned up the fields
And killed the overseers
They want freedom
And they want liberty

He thanked me verily
And made me get his gun
I did so quite quickly
All with a smile on my face

The master trusts me
He knows I am loyal
And I serve him well

So I give him the gun
And he runs to the field
But I laugh when I think
What time will reveal

For he went to stop the rebellion
With a gun in his hand
Little did he know
The gun I did provide
Has not a single bullet inside

WATCH THE EGO

Watch the ego
If it gets too big
It will be hard to carry
But you may learn this
Much too late
Egos are hard to carry
But easy to deflate

OBEAH

You are working obeah
Or something, I know
For you did not
Seem so attractive
Just a day ago

LEGBA

At the road
Between two realms
Is the guardian
An elder man
Who walks with a limp
Legba

Some say you are Satan
A devil
But I know you well
You are a great spirit
This I can tell

COLUMBUS

Christopher Columbus
Sailed the sea
He should have stayed
Stayed in Spain
Because he came to the Caribbean
And brought misery and pain

TYRANT

Tyrants
Beware
and live in fear
For the day the people
Become more aware

WAR

Rich men
Standing from afar
Sending young men
To fight wars

Hopes are shattered
Dreams are destroyed
And who wins
when people go to war?

THE ZOMBIE

The zombie
Is a creation
Of his master

The zombie
Is a slave
To his master

No mind of his own
No freedom to think

A zombie is a zombie
Among other zombies
And that is his comfort

BEWARE

Beware
When your neighbor
Falls
Because the road outside
Is difficult to walk
So if you see
That your neighbor fell
Beware
Beware
You may fall as well

SKINS

Although it pains me
This is true
That we are divided
Black African
And Brown African
And Yellow African

We share the same oppression
The same fate
But because of complexion of skin
Ourselves we came to hate

PA FÉ SA

They say
Pa fé sa
Don't do that
Do as we say
It's pa fé sa
Every night
And every day

But I will rebel
And do what I must
And all you critics
Will have to adjust

As much as you try
Still I move on
Because my rebellious slave spirit
Is much too strong

ADVICE

I asked Fred
For relationship
Advice
How to keep
My wife
In my life

I knew him well
For thirty years
And women problems
Were never his fears

Fred said to me
And I remember this well
To maintain a marriage
You must work like hell

TELLING ME TOO MUCH

People does get on my nerve
Telling me what to do
How to dress
How to think
What to think
What to value
Who to respect

But they never tell me
How to solve my problems
How to end poverty
How to be successful
How to be happy
They never tell me anything useful

CIVILIZATION

You judge civilization
By a flawed standard
So much technology
And buildings
And things
But what I see
Is people suffering
Loneliness
Poverty
Depression
And greed
These are the things
A civilization
Does not breed

GARDEN OF EDEN

What if we could
Change the history
Go back in time
And do things differently

I know what I would do
And you must believe
I would go to the Garden of Eden
With Adam and Eve

I would warn them
Of their potential mistake
I would make them save the fruit
And eat the snake

LEADERS

We know the athletes
We know the musicians
We know the comedians
We know the entertainers
But tell me
Tell me please
Who are our leaders?

HISTORY AND CULTURE

How can we survive
With no history
Or culture

A tree with no roots
Cannot survive
And a people with no roots
Will only strive
But never achieve

Our ancestors fought
To maintain those deep roots
So why today
Do we throw it away

IMPORTANT THINGS

Important things are never achieved
By focusing on insignificant problems

Change your focus
And you change what you achieve

PRESSURE

Imagine the pressure
There are a few seconds left
The ball is in your hand
Everything comes down to this
Will you succeed
Or fail

PROUD TED

Ted was proud
This he could not disguise
Because he was Black
But his wife has blue eyes

All over town
How he would boast
Because he was a Black man
But it's a white woman he loves the most

I asked him why
And this is what he said
He's proud of his identity
But he prefers white women instead

OUR ENSLAVEMENT

Took my language
Stole my culture
Our enslavement
Was a terrible fate
Robbed our identity
And left us with self-hate

MY PEOPLE

You come to my people
To rob us as you please
You beat
Rape
And oppress us
You brought us down to our knees

You took so many things
Our culture
Our land
Our gold rings

You rob of us of any identity
Language
Name
And history
Then turn around to further oppress we
On plantations in slavery

But I tell you this much
And you must listen well
I know my people
And under any condition we excel

Anything you give us
We survive
We faced so much different oppression
And we still thrive

OUR HOMELAND WILL BE FREE

(For Farida)

Torn apart
By slavery and oppression
But one day we will see
When our common homeland
Shall finally be free

Free from colonialism
And dictatorship
From poverty
And pain

Together we shall move mountains
And overcome everything in our way
To liberate our common motherland
To witness a brighter day

AGAINST ALL THE ODDS

If you stand for something
Prepare
Because on one side it is you
And on the other side
All the odds are there

I WORK

I work
With the hope
That one day
We shall succeed
Not me alone
But us
Together
Hand in hand

GOSSIP

When you gossip
Remember
Others gossip too
So the next set of gossip that you hear
May be gossip on you

CHEATER MAN VEX

Cheater man vex
So vex that he gone insane
Because he woman got wise
And beat he with he own game

CRITICS

I had critics
Who wanted to see me lose
But those critics left
When they walked in my shoes

SPOILER BEDBUG

An epidemic
Is spreading around the place
A spoiler bedbug
Biting woman on their face
And when they get bite
They get a curse
When they go to speak
They speak in reverse

Made in the USA
Middletown, DE
15 November 2020